Spanish

phrase book
for kids

AA

About this book

Jane Wightwick
had the idea

Wina Gunn
wrote the pages

Leila & Zeinah Gaafar
(aged 10 and 12) drew the
first pictures in each
chapter

Robert Bowers
(aged 56) drew the
other pictures, and
designed the book

Ana Bremon

did the Spanish stuff

Important things that **must** be included

© g-and-w Publishing 2008

Reprinted March 2009, January 2010 and April 2011

All rights reserved. This book may be used for private and personal use. This book or any part of it may not be reproduced or stored by any means or in any form. Inquiries related to any uses of this book should be directed to the Publisher.

A CIP catalogue record for this book is available from the British Library.

ISBNs: 978-0-7495-5991-5 (SS) and 25170931 (Aldi)

Published by AA Publishing, a trading name of AA Media Limited, whose registered office is Fanum House, Basing View, Basingstoke, Hampshire RG21 4EA. Registered number 06112600.

Colour separation by Keenes, Andover, UK

Printed and bound in China by Everbest

A04690

What's inside

Making friends

How to be cool with the group

Wanna play?

Our guide to joining in everything from hide-and-seek to the latest electronic game

Feeling hungry

Order your favourite foods or go local

Looking good

Make sure you keep up with all those essential fashions

Hanging out

At the pool, beach, or theme park—don't miss out on the action

Pocket money

Spend it here!

Grown-up talk

blah!
blah!
blah!
blah!

If you really, really have to!

Extra stuff

All the handy things— numbers, months, time, days of the week

my big brother
mi hermano mayor
👄 mee airmano my-yor

grandpa
abuelo
👄 abwelo

dad
papá
👄 pa-pah

grandma
abuela
👄 abwela

mum mamá
👄 ma-mah

my little sister
mi hermana pequeña
👄 mee airmana pekenya

MAKING FRIENDS

Half a step this way

stepfather/stepmother
padrastro/madrastra
👄 padrastro/madrastra

stepbrother/stepsister
hermanastro/hermanastra
👄 airmanastro/airmanastra

half-brother/half-sister
medio hermano/medio hermana
👄 medyo airmano/medyo airmana

Hi! ¡Hola!
👄 ola

What's your name?
¿Cómo te llamas?
👄 komo tay yamas

My name's ...
Me llamo ...
👄 may yamo

8

The Spanish put an upside-down question mark before a question, as well as one the right way up at the end. It's the same with exclamation marks.

¿Isn't that weird? ¡You bet!

from Canada
de Canadá
👄 day canadah

from Irelan
de Irlanda
👄 day eerlan

from Wales del País de Gales
👄 del pie-yis day gal-les

That means "the land of the Gau

from Scotland
de Escocia
👄 day escothya

from the U.S.
de los Estados Unidos
👄 day los estados
ooneedos

from England
de Inglaterra
👄 day eengla-tairra

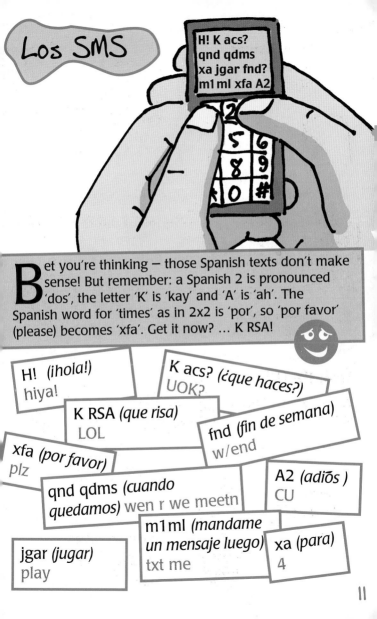

Los SMS

H! K acs?
qnd qdms
xa jgar fnd?
m1ml xfa A2

B et you're thinking – those Spanish texts don't make sense! But remember: a Spanish 2 is pronounced 'dos', the letter 'K' is 'kay' and 'A' is 'ah'. The Spanish word for 'times' as in 2x2 is 'por', so 'por favor' (please) becomes 'xfa'. Get it now? … K RSA!

H! *(¡hola!)*
hiya!

K acs? *(¿que haces?)*
UOK?

K RSA *(que risa)*
LOL

fnd *(fin de semana)*
w/end

xfa *(por favor)*
plz

qnd qdms *(cuando quedamos)* wen r we meetn

A2 *(adiōs)*
CU

m1ml *(mandame un mensaje luego)*
txt me

xa *(para)*
4

jgar *(jugar)*
play

How old are you?
¿Cuántos años tienes?
☜ kwantos anyos tee–enes

12 years old
Doce años ☜ dothay anyos

Happy birthday!
¡Cumpleaños feliz!
☜ koomplay–anyos faileeth

What's your star sign?
¿Qué signo del zodiaco eres?
☜ kay signo del thodee–ako air–res

When's your birthday?
¿Cuándo es tu cumpleaños?
☜ kwando es too koomplay–anyos

12

Star signs

AQUARIUS

Jan. 21 – Feb. 19
Acuario akwaree-o

PISCES

Feb. 20 – Mar. 20
Piscis pees-thees

ARIES

Mar. 21 – Apr. 20
Aries a-rees

TAURUS

Apr. 21 – May 21
Tauro towro

GEMINI

May 22 – June 21
Géminis hemeenees

CANCER

June 22 – July 23
Cáncer kanthair

LEO

July 24 – Aug. 23
Leo leo

VIRGO

Aug. 24 – Sep. 23
Virgo beergo

LIBRA

Sep. 24 – Oct. 23
Libra leebra

SCORPIO

Oct. 24 – Nov. 22
Escorpio eskorpee-o

SAGITTARIUS

Nov. 23 – Dec. 21
Sagitario sa-hee-taree-o

CAPRICORN

Dec. 22 – Jan. 20
Capricornio kapreecornee-o

14

football **el fútbol**
👄 el footbol

rollerblading
el patinaje en línea
👄 el patee-nahay en leenya

music
la música
👄 la mooseeka

electronic games
los juegos electrónicos
👄 los hway-gos elektroneekos

tv **la tele**
👄 la taylay

comics
los tebeos
👄 los taybayos

spiders **las arañas**
👄 las aranyas

school
el colegio
👄 el kolay-heeyo

15

What's your ...?

¿Cuál es tu ...?

👄 kwal es too ...

favourite group

grupo preferido

👄 groopo prefereedo

favourite colour

color preferido

👄 kol-lor prefereedo

→ Page 69

favourite game

juego preferido

👄 hway-go prefereedo

favourite food
comida preferida
☞ komeeda prefereeda

favourite ring tone
tono preferido
☞ tone-oh prefereedo

animal

favourite animal
animal preferido
☞ anee-mal prefereedo

favourite team
equipo preferido
☞ ekeepo prefereedo

17

Talk about your pets

He's hungry
Está hambriento
👄 esta ambree-yento

She's sleeping
Está durmiendo
👄 esta doormee-yendo

Can I stroke your dog?
¿Puedo acariciar tu perro?
👄 pwedo atharee-thyar too pair-ro

Do you have any pets?
¿Tienes alguna mascota?
👄 tee-enes algoona mascota

dog el perro
👄 el pair-ro

cat
el gato
👄 el gato

guinea-pig la cobaya
👄 la kob-eye-a

snake
la serpiente
👄 la serpee-entay

hamster
el hámster
👄 el hamstair

budgie
el periquito
👄 el peree-keeto

My little doggy goes *guau guau!*

A Spanish doggy (that's "guauguau" in baby language) doesn't say "woof, woof", it says *"guau, guau"* (*gwa-oo, gwa-oo*). A Spanish bird says *"pío, pío"* (*pee-o, pee-o*) and "cock-a-doodle-do" in Spanish chicken-speak is *"kikirikí"* (*kee-kee ree-kee*). But a cat does say *"miaow"* and a cow *"moo"* whether they're speaking Spanish or English!

19

Talk about school (if you can stand it)

geography
la geografía
👄 la heogra-feeya

art
el dibujo artístico
👄 el deebooho arteesteeko

PE
la gimnasia
👄 la heem-naseeya

maths las mates
👄 las mat-tes

Spanish
m.smith
form 2b

$\sqrt{E} + (.42 = \div x \div c^2$

Spanish
el español
👄 el espanyol

20

music
la música
👄 la mooseeka

English
el inglés
👄 el eeng-les

English
m. smith

I love Sandra
x
x

science
las naturales
👄 las natoorar-les

history
la historia
👄 la eestoreeya

21

IT
TI
👄 tay-ee

Way unfair!

Spanish children hardly ever have to wear uniform to school and have very long holidays: 10 weeks in the summer and another 5–6 weeks throughout the rest of the year. But before you turn green with envy, you might not like the mounds of "**deberes para las vacaciones**" (*debair-res para las bakathee-yones*), that's "vacation homework"! And if you fail your exams, the teachers could make you repeat the whole year with your little sister!

Talk about your phone

That's ancient!
¡Qué anticuado!
👄 kay antee-kwado

I've run out of credit
Me he quedado sin saldo
👄 may ay kaydado seen saldo

What's your mobile phone like?
¿Cómo es tu móvil?
👄 komo es too mo-beel

Lucky!
¡Qué suerte!
👄 kay swair-tay

What a cool ring tone!
¡Qué tono más chulo!
👄 kay tone-oh mass choolo

Gossip

Can you keep a secret?

¿Puedes guardar un secreto?

🗨 pwedes gwardar oon sekreto

Do you have a boyfriend (a girlfriend)?

¿Tienes novio (novia)?

🗨 tee-enes nobyo (nobya)

An OK guy/An OK girl

Un tío majo/Una tía maja

🗨 oon teeyo maho/oona teeya maha

What a bossy-boots!

¡Qué mandón!

🗨 kay man-don

He/She's nutty!

¡Está como una cabra!

🗨 esta komo oona kabra

That means "He/She's like a goat"!

"I'm not like that at all!"

What a misery-guts!

¡Qué malasombra!

🗨 kay malas-sombra

You won't make many friends saying this!

Bog off!
¡Vete a la porra!
👄 betay a la porra

Shut up! ¡Cállate!
👄 kigh-yatay

If you're fed up with someone, and you want to say something like "you silly …!" or "you stupid …!", you can start with **pedazo de** (which actually means "piece of …") and add anything you like. What about …

Stupid banana!
¡Pedazo de plátano!
(pedatho day platano)

or …

Silly sausage!
¡Pedazo de salchicha! *(pedatho day salcheecha)*

Take your pick. It should do the trick. You could also try **"¡pedazo de idiota!"** *(pedatho day eedee-ota)*. You don't need a translation here, do you?

You might have to say

Bother!
¡Ostras!
👄 os-stras

Rats! ¡Porras!
👄 porras

"Did someone call us?"

las ostras

That's not funny
No tiene gracia
👄 no tee-enay
gra-theeya

That's enough!
¡Ya vale!
👄 ya balay

I'm fed up
¡Estoy harto! (boys)
¡Estoy harta! (girls)
👄 estoy arto/estoy arta

26

Stop it!
¡No hagas eso!
👄 no agas eso

I want to go home!
¡Me quiero ir a casa!
👄 may kyairo eer ah kassa

I don't care
Me da igual
👄 may da eegwal

At last!
¡Por fin!
👄 por feen

27

Saying goodbye

Here's my address
Aquí tienes mi dirección
👄 akee tee-enes mee
deerek-thyon

What's your address?
¿Cuál es tu dirección?
👄 kwal es too deerek-thyon

Come to visit me
Ven a visitarme
👄 ben a
beesee-tarmay

Have a good trip!
¡Buen viaje!
👄 bwen bee-ahay

Write to me soon
Escríbeme pronto
👄 eskree-bemay pronto

Send me a text
Envíame un SMS
👄 envee-armay oon "SMS"

Shall we chat online?
¿Chateamos?
👄 chatay-amos

Bye!
¡Adiós!
👄 adeeyos

What's your email address?
¿Cuál es tu mail?
👄 kwal es too mail

⊃□@3♢*@ɳ.com

WANNA PLAY?

el elástico
👄 el elasteeko

el ping-pong
👄 el "ping-pong"

el reproductor
🙂 el raypro-
dooktor

el móvil
🙂 el mo-beel

el yo-yó
🙂 el "yo yo"

WANNA PLAY?

Do you want to play ...?
¿Quieres jugar ...?
👄 keyair-res hoogar

... table football?
... al futbolín?
👄 al footboleen

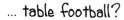

... cards?
... a las cartas?
👄 a las kartas

... on the computer?
... con el ordenador?
👄 kon el orden-ador

... noughts & crosses?
... a las tres en raya?
👄 a las trays en righ-ya

... hide-and-seek?
... al escondite?
👄 al eskon-deetay

... catch?
... al balón?
👄 al ballon

Not now.
Ahora no
👄 a-ora no

Yeah!
¡Vale!
👄 balay

Fancy a game of **foal** or **donkey**?!

In Spain, you don't play "leap frog", you play "foal" – *el potro*. There is also a group version of this called "donkey" – *el burro*. This involves two teams. Team 1 line up in a row with their heads down in the shape of a donkey. Team 2 take it in turns to leap as far as they can onto the back of the "donkey". If the donkey falls over, Team 2 win. If Team 2 touch the ground or can't leap far enough to get all the team on, then Team 1 win – got that?! Spanish children will try to tell you this is enormous fun, but your parents might not be so keen on the bruises!

Can my friend play too?
¿Mi amigo también puede jugar?
👄 mee ameego tam–byen pway–day hoogar

I have to ask my parents
Se lo tengo que pedir a mis padres
👄 say loe tengo ka pedeer ah mees padrau

34

Make yourself heard

Who dares?

You're it!
¡La quedas tú!
👄 la kedas too

Race you?
¿Una carrera?
👄 oona karraira

I'm first
Soy el primero (boys)
Soy la primera (girls)
👄 soy el preemairo
   soy la preemaira

Who's winning? ¿Quién gana?
keeyen gana

Ready, steady, go!
Preparados, listos, ¡ya!
pray-parados, leestos, yah

Where's the finish?
¿Dónde está la meta?
donday esta la mayta

I need a head start
Necesito ventaja
naythay-seeto benta-ha

37

Electronic games

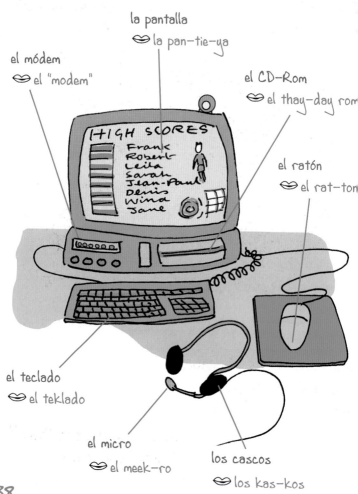

la pantalla
🗨 la pan-tie-ya

el módem
🗨 el "modem"

el CD-Rom
🗨 el thay-day rom

el ratón
🗨 el rat-ton

HIGH SCORES
Frank
Robert
Leila
Sarah
Jean-Paul
Denis
Wina
Jane

el teclado
🗨 el teklado

el micro
🗨 el meek-ro

los cascos
🗨 los kas-kos

Show me

Enséñame

 ensay-nyamay

Am I dead?

¿Me han matado?

👄 may an matado

What do I do?

¿Qué hay que hacer?

👄 kay eye kay athair

Shoot-em-up!

¡Dispárales!

👄 deespar-ralayz

How many lives do I have?

¿Cuántas vidas tengo?

👄 kwantas beedas tengo

How many levels are there?

¿Cuántos niveles hay?

👄 kwantos neebay-les eye

39

It's virtual fun!

Do you have a webcam?
¿Tienes una cámara web?
👄 tee-enes oona kam-ara web?

Send me a message.
Mándame un mensaje.

How do i join?
¿Cómo me apunto?

I'm not old enough.
No tengo edad suficiente.

I'm not allowed.
No tengo permiso.

I don't know who you are.
No te conozco.

my blog
mi blog
👄 mee blog

my friends
mis amigos
👄 mees ameegos

my photos
mis fotos
👄 mees fotos

my videos
mis videos
👄 mees bee-dayos

my music mi música
👄 mee mooseeka

41

Non couch-potato activities!

tennis
el tenis
👄 el tenees

trampolining
el trampolín
👄 el "trampoline"

bowling
los bolos
👄 los bol-los

swimming
la natación
👄 la nata-thyon

hockey
el hockey
👄 el "hockey"

gymnastics
la gimnasia
👄 la heem-nasya

ballet
el ballet
👄 el ballay

basketball el baloncesto
👄 el ballon-thesto

and, of course, we haven't forgotten *"el fútbol"* … (P.T.O.)

f⚽⚽tball

boots
las botas
👄 las botas

football kit
el equipo de fútbol
👄 el ekeepo day footbol

ref
el árbitro
👄 el arbeetro

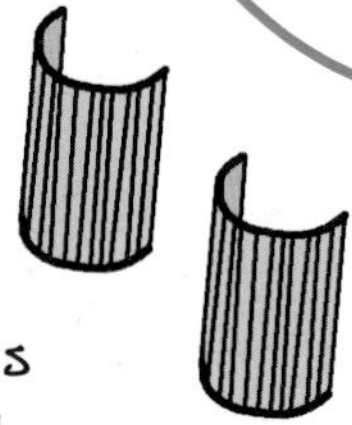

shin pads
las espinilleras
👄 las espinee-yeras

Good save!
¡Vaya parada!
👄 baya parada

Pass! ¡Pasa! 👄 pasa

Offside! ¡Offside!
☞ just say it!

Hands! ¡Mano!
☞ mano

You're in my team
Tú estás en mi equipo
☞ too estas en mee ekeepo

crossbar
el larguero
☞ el largairo

goalpost
el palo
☞ el pallo

goal el gol ☞ el gol

goalie
el portero
☞ el portairo

45

Keeping the others in line

Not like that!
¡Así no!
👄 asee no

You cheat!
¡Tramposo! (boys only)
¡Tramposa! (girls only)
👄 tramposo/tramposa

I'm not playing anymore
Ya no juego
👄 ya no hwego

Stop it!
¡No hagas eso!
👄 no agas eso

It's not fair!
¡No es justo!
👄 no es hoosto

Showing off

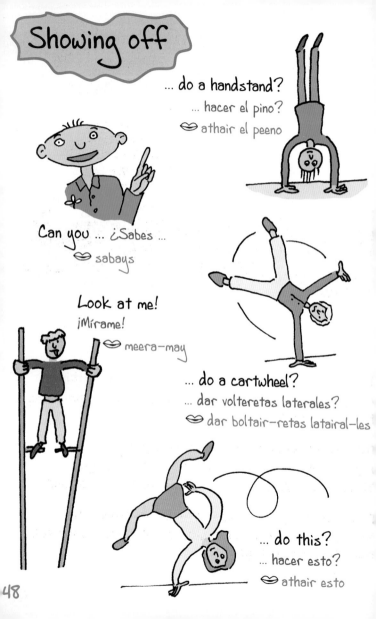

... do a handstand?
... hacer el pino?
👄 athair el peeno

Can you ... ¿Sabes ...
👄 sabays

Look at me!
¡Mírame!
👄 meera-may

... do a cartwheel?
... dar volteretas laterales?
👄 dar boltair-retas latairal-les

... do this?
... hacer esto?
👄 athair esto

48

Impress your Spanish friends with this!

You can show off to your new Spanish friends by practising this tongue twister:

Tres tristes tigres comían trigo en un trigal.
trays treestays teegrays comee-an treego en oon treegal
(This means "Three sad tigers ate wheat in a wheat field".)

Then see if they can do as well with this English one:
"She sells seashells on the seashore, but the shells she sells aren't seashells, I'm sure."

For a rainy day

pack of cards
una baraja de cartas
👄 oona baraha
   day kartas

my deal/your deal
yo doy/tú das
👄 yo doy/too das

king
el rey
👄 el ray

queen
la reina
👄 la ray-een

jack
la jota
👄 la hota

joker
el komodín
👄 el komodee

tréboles
👄 trebol-les

corazones
👄 korazon-nes

picas
👄 peekas

diamantes
👄 dee-amanta

50

Do you have the ace of swords?!

You might also see Spanish children playing with a different pack of cards. There are only 48 cards instead of 52 and the suits are also different. Instead of clubs, spades, diamonds and hearts, there are gold coins (*oros*), swords (*espadas*), cups (*copas*) and batons (*bastos*).

chessboard
el tablero
👄 el tablairo

el alfil
👄 el alfeel

peón
👄 el pay-on

el caballo
👄 el kab-eye-o

la torre 👄 la torray

la reina
👄 la ray-eena

el rey 👄 el ray

51

FEELING HUNGRY

hamburger
la hamburguesa
👄 la amboorgaysa

chips
las patatas fritas
👄 las patatas freetas

ice-crea[m]
el helado
👄 el elad[o]

coke
una coca
👄 oona koka

squid
los calamares
👄 los kalamar-res

reme caramel
el flan
👄 el flan
Watch out! "Flan" in
Spanish doesn't mean a
pastry tart with cheese!)

la paella
👄 la pie-eyya

orange juice
el zumo de naranja
👄 el thoomo day
naran-ha

Grub

I'm starving
Tengo un hambre de lobo
💋 tengo oon ambray day lobo

That means "I have the hunger of a wolf!"

el lobo

Please can I have ...
Por favor, me da ...
💋 por fabor, may da

... a croissant
un cruasán
👄 oon krwasan

... a cream bun
un bollo con nata
👄 oon boyo kon nata

... a puff pastry
una palmera
👄 oona palmayra

... a waffle
un gofre
👄 oon go-fray

... a muffin
una magdalena
👄 oona magda-layna

los churros
👄 los choorros

These are wonderful sugary doughnut-like snacks. They are sold in cafés and kiosks and usually come in a paper cone. They are also very popular for breakfast in winter with thick hot chocolate (**chocolate con churros**).

You: Can I have some churros, Mum?

Mum: No. They'll make you fat and rot your teeth.

You: But I think it's good to experience a foreign culture through authentic local food.

Mum: Oh, all right then.

Churros? *"¡Mm, mm!"*, Garlic sandwich? *"¡Agh!"*. If you're going to make foody noises you'll need to know how to do it properly in Spanish!

"Yum, yum!" is out in Spanish. You should say *"¡Mm, mm!"*. And "Yuk!" is *"¡Agh!"* (pronounced "ag"), but be careful not to let adults hear you say this!

... a lemonade
una Fanta®
de limón
👄 oona Fanta
day leemon

In Spain ask for
una Fanta® de limón
when you want a lemonade
or *Fanta® de naranja* (*fanta day naran-ha*) for a fizzy orange.
Fanta® is the most popular type
and so that's what people say.

... **water** agua
👄 agwa

... **a milkshake**
... un batido
👄 oon bateedo

You get your hot
chocolate in a large
cup (to dunk your
churros in).

... **a hot chocolate**
... un chocolate
👄 oon chokolatay

How did you like it?

That's lovely
Eso está super bueno
👄 eso esta soopair bweno

That's gorgeous
Eso está delicioso
👄 eso esta daylee-
thee-oso

I don't like that
Eso no me gusta
👄 eso no may goosta

I'm stuffed
Voy a explotar
👄 boy a explotar

I can't eat that
No me lo puedo comer
👄 no may lo pwedo komair

That's gross
Está asqueroso
👄 esta askairoso

Tap into *Tapas*

There's a perfect way to try a little bit of everything in Spain and that's *"tapas"*. These are little snacks that everyone eats in cafés and bars (which the adults might insist on going to).

Tapas come in little dishes and are a great way of finding out if you like something without risking a torrent of abuse if you leave an expensive meal untouched.

Here are four of the most popular:

tortilla
👄 tortee-ya

Spanish omelette – thick and comes in slices

croquetas
👄 kroketas

egg-shaped rissoles filled with chicken, ham or fish

albóndigas
👄 albon-deegas

meatballs in tomato sauce

calamares a la romana
👄 kalamar-res a la romana

squid rings

Parties

balloon el globo
👄 el glow-bo

Can I have some more?
¿Puedo tener un poco más?
👄 pwaydo tenair oon poko mas

party hat
el gorro de fiesta
👄 el gorro day fee-esta

This is for you
Esto es para ti
👄 esto es para tee

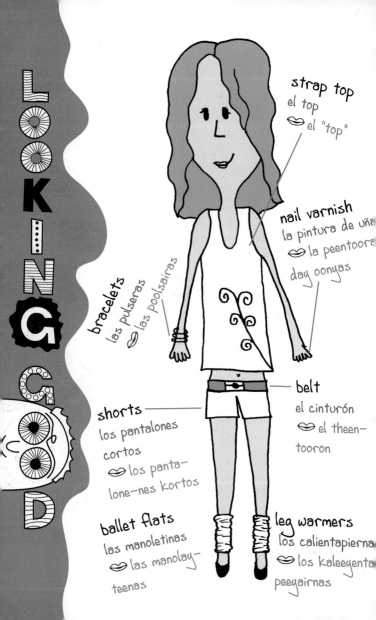

LOOKING GOOD

strap top
el top
👄 el "top"

nail varnish
la pintura de uña
👄 la peentoora
day oonyas

bracelets
las pulseras
👄 las poolsairas

belt
el cinturón
👄 el theen-
tooron

shorts
los pantalones
cortos
👄 los panta-
lone-nes kortos

ballet flats
las manoletinas
👄 las manolay-
teenas

leg warmers
los calientapierna
👄 los kaleeyenta
peeyairnas

cap la gorra
🖉 la gorra

hoodie
la capucha
🖉 la kapoocha

tattoo
la calcomanía
🖉 la kalko-maneeya

jeans
los vaqueros
🖉 los bakayros

trainers
las deportivas
🖉 las daypor-teebas

LOOKING GOOD

That T-shirt please
Esa camiseta, por favor
👄 esa kameeseta, por fabor

Cool tattoo!
¡Qué calcamonía más chula!
👄 kay kalka-moneeya mass choola

The pink frilly one
👄 La rosa con volantitos
👄 la rosa kon bolanteetos

Awesome miniskirt!
¡Vaya minifalda mas chula!
👄 baya meenee falda
mass choola

The purple stripey one
La morada de rayas
👄 la morada day righ-yas

spotty
de lunares
👄 day loonar-res

flowery de flores
👄 day flor-res

frilly
con volantitos
👄 kon bolanteetos

glittery
con brillos
👄 kon breeyos

stripey
de rayas
👄 day righ-yas

65

Clothes

jeans
los vaqueros
👄 los bakayros

sweatshirt
la sudadera
👄 la sooda dayra

T-shirt
la camiseta
👄 la kameeseta

football shirt
la camiseta de fútbol
👄 la kameeseta day footbol

trainers
las deportivas
👄 las daypor-teebas

shoes los zapatos
👄 los thapatos

skirt
la falda
👄 la falda

dress
el traje
👄 el trahay

trousers
los pantalones
👄 los panta-lone-nes

A pair of cowboys?

The word for jeans in Spanish (*los vaqueros* – *los bakayros*) actually means "cowboys" because they were the first people to wear these trousers.

Make it up!

lip gloss
el Brillo de lab[...]
☞ el breeyo da[...]
labyos

glitter gel
la brillantina
☞ la breeyan—teena

nail varnish
el pintauñas
☞ el peentaw—
nyas

earrings los pendientes
☞ los pend—yentays

I need a mirror
Necesito un espejo
☞ netthayseeto oon
espay-ho

eye shadow
la sombra de ojos
☞ la sombray day o-hos

Can I borrow
your straighteners?
¿Me dejas tu alisador
de pelo? ☞ may day-
has too alee-sadoor day pay-lo

68

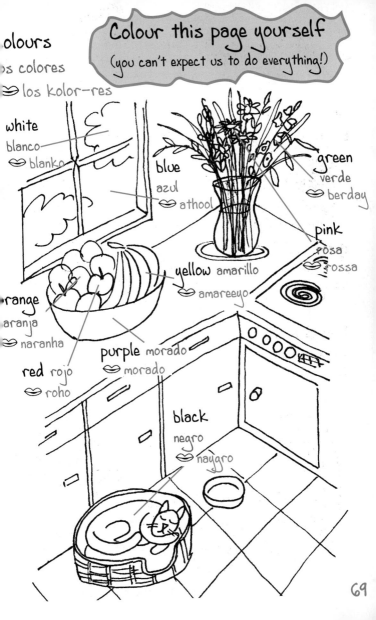

olours

los colores
👄 los kolor-res

Colour this page yourself
(you can't expect us to do everything!)

white
blanco
👄 blanko

blue
azul
👄 athool

green
verde
👄 berday

pink
rosa
👄 rossa

yellow amarillo
👄 amareeyo

orange
naranja
👄 naranha

purple morado
👄 morado

red rojo
👄 roho

black
negro
👄 naygro

69

What shall we do?
¿Qué hacemos?
👄 kay athay-mos

Can I come?
¿Puedo ir?
👄 pwedo eer

Where do you lot hang out?
¿Por dónde salís vosotros?
👄 por donday salees bos-otros

That's really wicked
Eso es chachi
👄 eso es chachee

I'm (not) allowed
(No) me dejan
👄 (no) may day-han

Let's go back Regresemos
☞ regray-saymos

That gives me goose bumps (or "chicken flesh" in Spanish!)
Eso me pone la carne de gallina
☞ eso may ponay la karnay day gayeena

I'm bored to death
muero de aburrimiento
☞ may mwero day aburree-mee-ento

HOUSE OF MIRRORS

That's a laugh
Te ríes cantidad
☞ tay reeyes kanteedad

73

Beach babies

Can I borrow this?
¿Me dejas esto?
🗣 may dehas esto

Is this your bucket?
¿Es tuyo este cubo?
🗣 es tooyo estay koobo

Stop throwing sand!
¡Deja de echar arena!
🗣 dayha day echar arayna

Let's hit the beach
Vamos a la playa
🗣 bamos a la playa

You can bury me
Me puedes enterrar
🗣 pay pwedes entair-rar

Mind my eyes!
¡Cuidado con mis ojos!
🗣 kweedado kon mees ohos

74

sandcastle
castillo de arena
👄 el casteeyo day arayna

sea el mar
👄 el mar

beach
la playa
👄 la playa

towel
la toalla
👄 la toe–aya

swimming costume
el bañador
👄 el banyador

snorkel
el tubo
👄 el toobo

bucket el cubo
👄 el koobo

spade
la pala
👄 la palla

shells
las conchas
👄 las konchas

75

It's going swimmingly!

How to make a splash in Spanish!

PLOF

Let's hit the swimming pool
Vamos a la piscina
👄 bamos a la peeseena

Can you swim (underwater)
¿Sabes nadar (debajo del agua)
👄 sabays nadar (debaho del agwa)

Me too/ I can't
Yo también/Yo no
👄 yo tambeeyen/ yo no

Can you dive?
¿Te sabes tirar de cabeza?
👄 tay sabays teerar day kabaytha

I'm getting changed

Me estoy cambiando
👄 may estoy kambee-ando

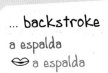

... backstroke
a espalda
👄 a espalda

Can you swim ...?
¿Sabes nadar ...?
👄 sabays nadar

... butterfly
a mariposa
👄 a mareeposa

... crawl
a crol
👄 a krol

... breaststroke
a braza 👄 a bratha

slide
el tobogán
👄 el tobogan

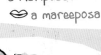

goggles
las gafas
👄 las gafas

77

Downtown

Do you know the way?
¿Te sabes el camino?
👄 tay sabays el kameeno

Let's ask
Vamos a preguntar
👄 bamos a pray-goontar

Pooper-scoopers on wheels!

You might see bright green-and-white motorcycles with funny vacuum cleaners on the side riding around town scooping up the dog poop. The people riding the bikes look like astronauts! (Well, you'd want protection too, wouldn't you?)

bus
el autobús
👄 el owtoboos

Is it far? ¿Está lejos?
👄 esta lay-hos

car el coche
👄 el kochay

Are we allowed in here?
¿Nos dejan entrar aquí?
👄 nos day-han entrar akee

You could gain a lot of street cred with your new Spanish friends by using a bit of slang. A clapped-out car is **"una cafetera"** (*oona cafaytayra*), which means "coffee pot"! Try this: **"¡Vaya cafetera!"** (*baya cafaytayra* – "What an old banger!").

Park yourself here

swings los columpios
👄 los koloom-peeyos

climbing frame
el juego para escalar
👄 el hway-go para
eska-lar

playground
el patio de recreo
👄 el pateeyo day rekrayo

grass la hierba
👄 la yairba

tree el árbol
👄 el ar-bol

slide
el tobogán
👄 el tobogan

park el parque 👄 el parkay

Can we play ball games?

¿Podemos jugar a la pelota?

poday-mos hoo-gar a la pay-lota

roundabout

el tiovivo

el tio-beebo

sandpit el arenero

el arain-airo

Can I have a go?

¿Puedo intentarlo?

pwaydo
intain-tarloe

81

Picnics

I hate wasps
Odio las avispas
👄 odeeyo las
 abeespas

Move over!
¡Apártate!
👄 apar–tatay

bread el pan
👄 el pan

Shall we sit here?
¿Nos sentamos aquí?
👄 nos sentamos akee

napkin
la servilleta
👄 la serbeeyeta

ham el jamón
👄 el hamon

cheese
el queso
👄 el kayso

yoghurt
el yogurt
👄 el yogurt

crisps
las patatas fritas
👄 las patatas
 freetas

drinks
las bebidas
👄 las bebeedas

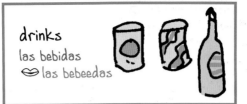

knife
el cuchillo
👄 el koocheeyo

spoon
la cuchara
👄 la koochara

wasps
las avispas
👄 las abeespas

fork
el tenedor
👄 el tenaydor

bees
las abejas
👄 las abayhas

bzzzz

ants
las hormigas
👄 las ormeegas

Wake up, campers!

tent la tienda
👄 la tyen-da

tent peg la pique
👄 la pee-kayta

camper van
la caravana
👄 la kara-vana

penknife
la navaja de bolsillo
👄 la nava-ha day
bol-seelyo

camping stove
el camping gas
👄 el "camping gas"

sleeping bag el saco de dormir
👄 el sak-ko day door-meer

torch la linterna
👄 la lintair-na

That tent's a palace! Jo, ¡vaya tienda!
👄 ho, buy-ya tyen-da

Is there a
campfire?
¿Hay una hoguera?
👄 ay oona og-waira

I've lost my torch
He perdido mi linterna
👄 eh pairdeedo mee
lintair-na

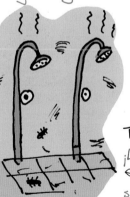

The showers are gross
¡Las duchas están sucias!
👄 las doo-chas estan
soothyas

Where does the rubbish go?
¿Dónde se tira la basura?
👄 donday say teera la basoora

85

All the fun of the fair

helter-skelter
el tobogán 👄 el tobogan

big wheel
la noria
👄 la noreeya

house of mirrors
la casa de
los espejos 👄 la kasa day los espayhos

dodgems
los coches de choque
👄 los kochays
day chokay

Shall we go on this?
¿Nos montamos en éste?
👄 nos montamos en estay

86

Disco nights

mirror ball
la bola de espejos
👄 la bola day espay-hos

loudspeaker
el altavoz
👄 el altab-oth

Can I request a song?
¿Puedo pedir una canción?
👄 pwaydo paydeer oona kan-thyon

The music is really lame
¡La música es malísima!
👄 la mooseeka es malee-seema

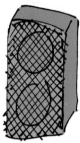

DJ
el pinchadiscos
👄 el peencha-deeskos

spotlights
los focos
👄 los fo-ko

turntable
el tocadiscos
👄 el toka-deeskos

How old do I need to be?

¿Cuántos años hay que tener?

👄 kwantos anyos ay kay tenair

dance floor

la pista de baile

👄 la peesta day balay

Let's dance!

¡Vamos a bailar!

👄 ba-mos a balar

I love this song!

¡Me encanta esta canción!

👄 may enkanta esta kan-thyon

P O C K E T M O N E Y

sweets
los caramelos
👄 los karamaylos

T-shirts
las camisetas
👄 las kameese*

toys los juguetes
👄 los hoogetes

el tendero
👄 el tenday*

books
los libros
 los leebros

el móvil
los mobeel

pencils los lápices
los lapeethes

What does that sign say?

carnicería
butcher shop
👄 karneethereeya

pastelería
cake shop
👄 pasteler
—reeya

panadería
bakery
👄 panadereeya

confitería
sweet shop
👄 confeeter—
reeya

papelería
stationers
👄 papelereeya

verdulería
grocery shop
👄 berdooler—
reeya

boutique
clothes shop
👄 booteek

Do you have some dosh?
¿Tienes pasta?
👄 tee-enes pasta

I'm skint
No tengo un duro
👄 no tengo oon dooro

I'm loaded
Estoy forrado
👄 estoy forrado

Here you go
Aquí tienes
👄 akee tee-enes

That's a weird shop!
¡Vaya tienda más rara!
👄 buy-ya tyen-da mas ra-ra

That's a bargain
Eso es una ganga
👄 eso es oona ganga

It's a rip off
Es un robo
👄 es oon robo

93

Sweet heaven!

I love this shop
Me encanta esta tienda
👄 may enkanta esta tee-enda

Let's get some sweets
Vamos a comprar chucherías
👄 bamos a comprar choochereeyas

Let's get an ice-cream
Vamos por un helado
👄 bamos por oon aylado

lollipops las piruletas
👄 las peerooletas

a bar of chocolate
una tableta de chocolate
👄 oona tableta day chokolat[a]

chewing gum el chicle
👄 el cheeklay

If you really want to look Spanish and end up with lots of fillings ask for:

regaliz (regaleez)
soft licorice sticks, available in red or black

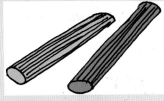

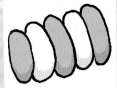

nubes (noobes)
soft marshmallow sweets ("flumps") in different shades (*nubes* means clouds)

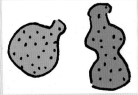

jamones (hamon-nes)
fruity, fizzy gums in the shape of hams ("ham" is *jamón*)

Chupa-chups® (choopa-choops)
lollies famous all over the world, but they come from Spain

polvos pica-pica (polvos peeka peeka)
tangy fizzy sherbet sold in small packets with a lollipop to dip in

kilométrico (keelomay-treeko)
chewing gum in a strip like dental floss – pretend to the adults that you're flossing your teeth!

Other things you could buy

(that won't rot your teeth!)

What are you getting?
¿Qué te vas a comprar?
👄 kay tay bas a komprar

That toy, please
Ese juguete, por favor
👄 esay hoogetay, por fabor

Two postcards, please
Dos postales, por favor
👄 dos postal-les, por fabor

This is rubbish
Esto es una porquería
👄 esto es oona porkayreeya

This is cool
Esto mola
👄 esto mola

I'm getting ...

Voy a comprar
👄 boy a comprar

... a pen
... un boli
👄 oon bolee

... stamps
... sellos
👄 seyos

. felt tip pens
. rotuladores
👄 rotoolador-res

... colouring pencils
... lápices de colores
👄 lapeethes day kolor-res

.. a key ring
.. un llavero
👄 oon yabairo

... comics
... tebeos
👄 taybayos

... a shell box
... un joyero de conchas
☺ oon ho-yairo day konchas

... a fridge magnet
... un imán de nevera
☺ oon ee-man day nay-baira

How much is that?
¿Cuánto cuesta?
☺ kwanto kwesta

... a CD
... un compact
☺ oon compact

For many years Spain's favourite comics have been *Mortadelo y Filemón*, two accident-prone TIA agents (<u>not</u> CIA) and *Zipi y Zape*, two very naughty twins. Children also like to read *Mafalda*, an Argentinian comic, *Carlitos y Snoopy* (Charlie Brown & Snoopy), *Tintin*, *Astérix* and *¿Dónde está Wally?* (Where's Wally?).

Money talks

How much pocket money do you get?

¿Cuánto te dan de paga?

👄 kwanto tay dan day pa-ga

I only have this much

Sólo tengo esto

👄 soul-lo tain-go esto

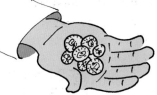

Can you lend me 10 euros?

¿Me prestas diez euros?

👄 may praystas deeyeth ay-ooros

No way!

¡Ni hablar!

👄 nee ablar

Money talk

Spanish money is the **euro** (pronounced *ay-ooro*).
A euro is divided into 100 **centimos** (*thainteemos*).

Coins: 1, 2, 5, 10, 20, 50 **centimos**

1, 2 **euros**

Notes: 5, 10, 20, 50, 100 **euros**

Make sure you know how much you are spending before you blow all your pocket money at once!

GROWN UP TALK

It hurts here
Me duele aquí
may dwaylay akee

bump
el chichón
el cheechon

plaster
la tirita
la teereeta

child
niño (boy)/niña (girl)
neenyo/neenya

GROWN UP TALK

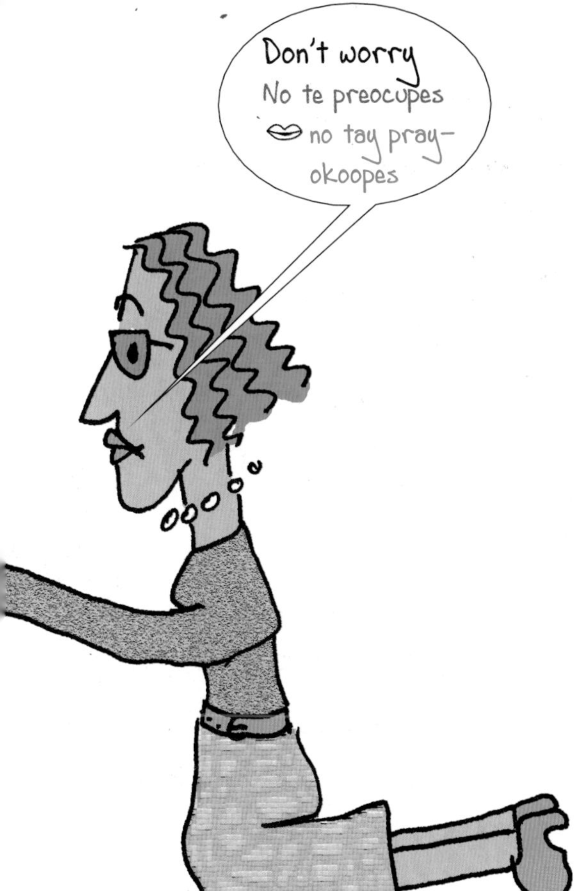

grown-up
adulto
adoolto

Help!

Something has dropped/broken
Algo se ha caído/roto
👄 algo say a kigh-eedo/roto

Please
Por favor
👄 por fabor

Can you help me?
¿Me puedes ayudar?
👄 may pwedes ayooda

Where's the letter box?
¿Dónde está el buzón?
👄 donday esta el boothon

Where are the toilets?
¿Dónde están los aseos?
👄 donday estan los asayos

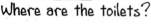

102

I can't manage it
No puedo
👄 no pwedo

Could you pass me that?
¿Me pasas eso?
👄 may pasas eso

What's the time?
¿Qué hora es?
👄 kay ora es

Come and see
Ven a ver
👄 ben a bair

May I look at your watch?
¿Me deja que mire su reloj?
👄 may deha kay meera soo reloh

Lost for words

... **my ticket**
mi billete
👄 mee beeyaytay

I've lost ...
He perdido ...
👄 eh perdeedo

... **my mobile**
mi móvil
👄 mee
mo-beel

... **my parents**
mis padres
👄 mees padrays

... **my shoes**
mis zapatos
👄 mees thapatos

... **my money** mi dinero
👄 mee deenayro

... **my jumper**
mi jersey
👄 mee hersay

... **my watch**
mi reloj
👄 mee reloh

... **my jacket** mi chaqueta
👄 mee chakayta

105

ADULTS ONLY!

Show this page to adults who can't seem to make themselves clear (it happens). They will point to a phrase, you read what they mean, and you should all understand each other perfectly.

No te preocupes
Don't worry

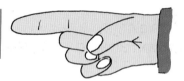

Siéntate aquí
Sit down here

¿Tu nombre y apellidos?
What's your name and surname?

¿Cuántos años tienes?
How old are you?

¿De dónde eres?
Where are you from?

¿Dónde te alojas?
Where are you staying?

¿Dónde te duele?
Where does it hurt?

¿Eres alérgico a algo?
Are you allergic to anything?

Está prohibido
It's forbidden

Tiene que acompañarte un adulto
You have to have an adult with you

Voy por alguien que hable inglés
I'll get someone who speaks English

EXTRA STUFF

weather
el tiempo
el tyem-po

numbers los números los noo

time
la hora
👄 la ora

Knock, knock.

Who's there?

Uno.

Uno who?

Unos where I got this crummy joke!

uno   💋 oono

1

dos   💋 dos

2

tres   💋 trays

3

cuatro   💋 kwatro

4

cinco   💋 theenko

5

seis   💋 sayis

110 6

ete
see-etay
7

ocho
ocho
8

Jeve
nwebay
9

iez
deeyeth
10

nce
onthay
11

loce
dothay
12

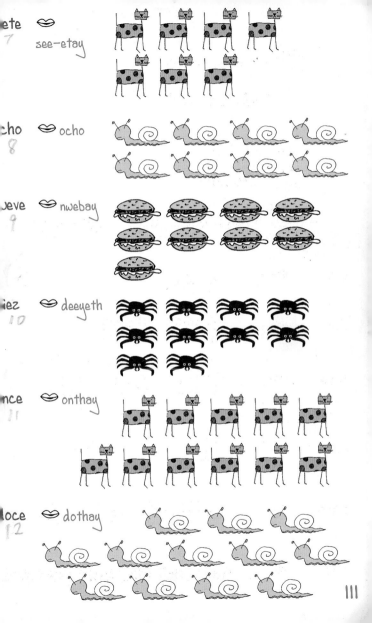

trece 👄 trethay
13

catorce 👄 katorthay
14

quince 👄 keenthay
15

16	dieciséis	*deeyethee sayis*
17	diecisiete	*deeyethee see-etay*
18	dieciocho	*deeyethee ocho*
19	diecinueve	*deeyethee nueboy*

If you want to say "twenty-two", "sixty-five" and so on, you can just put the two numbers together like you do in English. But don't forget to add the word for "and" (**y** – *ee*) in the middle:

32	**treinta y dos**	*traynta ee dos*
54	**cincuenta y cuatro**	*theenkwenta ee kwatro*
81	**ochenta y uno**	*ochenta ee oono*

20	Veinte	*beynte*
30	treinta	*traynta*
40	cuarenta	*kwarenta*
50	cincuenta	*theenkwenta*
60	sesenta	*saysenta*
70	setenta	*saytenta*
80	ochenta	*ochenta*
90	noventa	*nobenta*
100	cien	*theeyen*

1,000 mil *meel*

a million *un millón oon meel-yon*

a gazillion! *tropecientos! tropay- theeyentos*

1st	primero	*preemairo*
2nd	segundo	*segoondo*
3rd	tercero	*terthayro*
4th	cuarto	*kwarto*
5th	quinto	*keento*
6th	sexto	*sexto*
7th	séptimo	*septeemo*
8th	octavo	*octabo*
9th	noveno	*nobayno*
10th	décimo	*daytheemo*

Fancy a date?

I f you want to say a date in Spanish, you don't need to use 1st, 2nd, etc. Just say

Lunes	Martes	Miércoles	Jueves	Viernes	Sábado	Domingo
		1	2	3	4	5
6	7	8	9	10	11	12
13	14	15	16	17	18	19
20	21	22	23	24	25	26
27	28	29	30			

the ordinary number followed by **de** (*day*):

uno de marzo   (1st of March)

diez de julio   (10th of July)

March	marzo	*martho*
April	abril	*abreel*
May	mayo	*my-yo*

June	junio	*hooneeyo*
July	julio	*hooleeyo*
August	agosto	*agosto*

September	septiembre	*septee-embray*
October	octubre	*octoobray*
November	noviembre	*nobee-embray*

December	diciembre	*deethee-embray*
January	enero	*enayro*
February	febrero	*febrayro*

primavera *preemabayra*

SPRING

verano *berano*

SUMMER

otoño *otonyo*

AUTUMN

invierno *eenbee-erno*

WINTER

Monday	lunes	*loon-nes*
Tuesday	martes	*mar-tes*
Wednesday	miércoles	*mee-erkol-les*
Thursday	jueves	*hoo-ebes*
Friday	viernes	*bee-er-nes*
Saturday	sábado	*sabado*
Sunday	domingo	*domeengo*

By the way, Spanish kids have a two-and-a-half hour lunch break! Time enough for lunch and a siesta. But they don't finish until 5pm in the afternoon.

Good times

It's ...
Son ...
👄 sonn

(five) o'clock
las (cinco)
👄 las (theenko)

quarter past (two)
las (dos) y cuarto
👄 las (dos) ee kwarto

quarter to (four)
las (cuatro) menos cuarto
👄 las (kwatro) menos kwarto

half past (three)
las (tres) y media
👄 las (trays) ee medya

five past (ten)
las (diez) y cinco
👄 las (deeyeth) ee
theenko

twenty past (eleven)
las (once) y viente
👄 las (onthay) ee
baintay

ten to (four)
las (cuatro) menos diez
👄 las (kwatro) menos
deeyeth

twenty to (six)
las (seis) menos veinte
👄 las (sayis) menos
baintay

W atch out for "one o'clock". It's a bit different from the other times. If you want to say "It's one o'clock" you have to say **_Es la una_** (*es la oona*). "It's half past one" is **_Es la una y media_** (*es la oona ee medya*), and so on.

121

morning
mañana
👄 la manyarna

midday mediodía
👄 el medyo-deeya

afternoon la tarde
👄 la tarday

evening la noche
👄 la nochay

midnight
la medianoche
👄 la medya-nochay

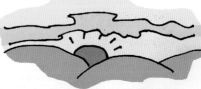

122

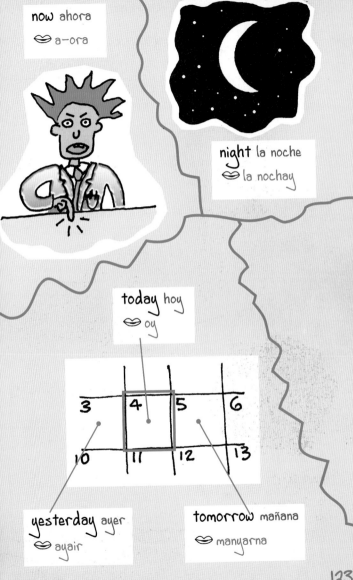

123

Weather wise

Can we go out?
¿Podemos salir fuera?
👄 podaymos saleer fwer

It's hot
Hace calor
👄 athay kalor

It's cold
Hace frío 👄 athay freeyo

It's a horrible day
Hace un día horrible
👄 athay oon deeya orreebl

It's raining seas!

In Spanish it doesn't rain "cats and dogs", it rains "seas"! That's what they say when it's raining really heavily:
¡Está lloviendo a mares!
esta yobeeyendo a mar-res

124

It's windy
Hace viento
👄 athay beeyento

It's sunny
Hace sol
👄 athay sol

It's raining
Está lloviendo
👄 esta yobeeyendo

It's snowing
Está nevando
👄 esta nebando

It's nice
Hace bueno
👄 athay bweno

I'm soaked
Estoy empapado
👄 estoy empapardo

125

Signs of life

altura mínima
minimum height

Móviles
prohibidos
No mobiles

Entrada prohibida
No entry

Sólo mayores
de 18
Over 18s only

Sólo menores de 5
Under 5s only